NEU Gen Leaders

Secrets of Academic Excellence

Ugo Njoku

NEU Gen Leaders:

Secrets of Academic Excellence

ISBN: 9780578447544

Copyright © 2018 by NEU Gen Leaders

Printed in the United States of America

NEU Gen Leaders Contact:

Phone: +1(317) 969-7092

email: neugenleaders1@gmail.com

Website: www.neugenleaders.com

Social Media: @neugenleaders

Editor
Chidiebere 'Chichi' Eze
email: cbereze@gmail.com

All rights reserved. In accordance with the U.S. Copyright Act of 1976, the scanning, uploading, and electronic sharing of any part of this book without the permission of the publisher constitute unlawful piracy and theft of the author's intellectual property. If you would like to use material from the book (other than for review purposes), prior written permission must be obtained by contacting the publisher at the email address listed above. Thank you for your support of the author's rights.

DEDICATION

To my wife, Elizabeth; your support fuels my ambition. You'll always be the biggest jackpot I won in life. I love you.

CONTENTS

Introduction viiii

Chapter One: Why Bother? 3

Chapter Two: Setting Goals 155

Chapter Three: Keeping Score 31

Chapter Four: Don't Just Read...Study 43

Chapter Five: Embrace Your Textbook! 89

Acknowledgements 113

About the author 115

INTRODUCTION

Welcome! I'm glad you've decided to take on this challenge to turn your academic performance around or push it up some more! You're a unique individual for deciding to take action. I say that because, even though you might have been forced to read this book, or you might have very well picked it up on your own, no one can really force you to do what you don't want to do. So, the fact that you're reading this says so much about your commitment to excel academically; and for that, I applaud you!

Here's one thing I know for sure: *everyone is smart!* Every single individual is smart...and you're no exception. All you need is the right kind of motivation to dig in your heels and work on the areas where you're slacking. For some people, it's studying; for others, it's making the right kind of friends, or learning to be more organized. But no matter the areas where you're slacking, the one thing I know for sure is this: *you're smart...waay smarter than you currently are. And I'll show you just how to unveil it.*

Anybody who wants to turn their academic career around can use this book. There are lessons and tricks that have helped many students – both those in high school and college alike – discussed in detail. I, for one, wasn't particularly book smart before my high school days. I wasn't dumb either; I just wasn't motivated. But applying the techniques in this book helped me to graduate with honors from high school, college/university and post-graduate studies. So, how do you turn an unmotivated student into an A student, you ask? Well, read on...

So, as we take this journey together, take my ideas, interpret them in the manner that best suits you, and then apply them. Let's work together. Please don't read this book passively. The lessons in here will benefit you only if you go beyond merely reading, to applying. Remember there are no magic formulas – only tested and proven practices. Even though I can't make your wish come true (I never said I was a thousand-year-old genie!), I only know that the ideas I've written down will benefit you if you put them into practice as I've written them. If you decide to tweak them a little to suit your personality and then put them into practice, they would work just as well.

A Special Note to Middle/High School Students

If you're in middle or high school and happen to be reading this book, please don't feel intimidated by the information and the ideas that would be discussed. I realize that you may not be required to study as hard – if at all – in high school. However, remember that college is not nearly as easy or "fly-by" as high school.

In college, no one spoon feeds you the information you're supposed to know. The lecturers are mostly very occupied with their research and publications that they may not have too much time to "babysit" as much as your teachers did in high school. There are certain information they expect that you should have known before coming into their class; and others, they expect you to look up by yourself in preparation for lectures and your exams. As a matter of fact, some schools would rather have you fail than succeed! Because, the more you fail, the more you'd have to pay tuition to retake those classes. Don't forget that your college – irrespective of its reputation – is still a business. And businesses are set up to make profit, amongst other things!

Learning and practicing the principles we talk about in this book will be very beneficial to you – both now and in the future. It will help you prepare for what is ahead. It will arm you with the techniques you'll need to excel in college and beyond. So, don't feel left out; take this amazing journey with the rest of us. Remember you'll get to college someday.

Finally, in the beginning of each chapter is a key question intended to focus your mind on the main subject covered in that chapter. We hope this helps you get the most out of this book.

- Ugo Njoku

"Never let the future disturb you. You will meet it, if you have to, with the same weapons of reason which today arm you against the present."

- Marcus Aurelius

Key Question:

- What is motivating you to do well in school?

2　　　　　　　　　　　WHY BROTHER?

Chapter One

Why Bother?

We Operate by Reason

I would like us to start by examining the foundation of our actions a little. "Reasons" is the fuel that drives our decision making and hence, our actions. We are constantly looking for reasons to justify our actions – i.e. before taking any action, we consciously or subconsciously look for the answer to the question, "Why must I do this?". If enough reasons are found in favour of the action, we'll take it. If not, we'll back away from it.

For instance, what we just described above is why you don't listen to some people's suggestions on an issue but pay close attention to others. It's because your brain has determined that they've earned your respect and, therefore, deserve to be heard.

Have you ever caught yourself doing something incredibly outrageous? I mean...something you wouldn't do on a very good day. Like talking on the phone at 3AM in the morning? Or talking on the phone for about six hours straight? Or worst still, walking for miles to a girl's house just to save on some money to take her out? I mean...incredibly outrageous things that you wouldn't do for just about anybody. I'd be lying if I said I haven't done any of those things; and you'd be lying if you didn't agree with me. Would you like to know *why* you did those things? It's because you felt "something" for the person; and, therefore, concluded that he/she was worth it.

So, we're constantly asking ourselves "Why?" Why listen? Why bother talking or trying? Why write? (I had to do a lot of this one!) Why study?

This is why this chapter is so important; because we are going to discuss this subject – "*why* should you study?" It's important that we do, because when you give someone enough "Why's," you can motivate him to do incredible things. And remember, once we find enough reasons to justify any action, we'll take it...always!

Reasons for Academic Excellence

Here are some of the reasons why I think it's very crucial that you take this journey of academic excellence to the end:

1. God expects you to:

I am an adamant believer that God never meant for us, as Christians, to be losers. I believe Christianity is not a religion, but a relationship with God – our Father. I believe this relationship transforms every area of our lives in a very remarkable way. I believe Christianity – the way God intended it – is very practical!

God expects us to display His glory in the world by our fruits, i.e. by the outward expressions of our lives. So, I don't agree with those Christians who choose only to pray, but refuse to study believing that God will miraculously appear and help them pass...with A's. Now, if they truly prayed and listened to God, they'd hear Him say, "Get your lazy bum up and go study!"

Now, on a more serious note, in John 14:26, Jesus said "But the Helper, the Holy Spirit, whom the Father will send in My name, He will teach you all things, and bring to your remembrance all things that I said to you." Here, Jesus was describing some characteristics of the Holy Spirit. He said **the Holy Spirit will teach us all things**, and **He will also remind us of things**. In that verse Jesus was telling His disciples that the Holy Spirit will remind them of the things He said to them. But remember that this is a characteristic of His. It is His "character" – i.e. His personality and fundamental quality.

So, it doesn't really matter what it is; Physics, Chemistry, Science, Mathematics, English, Statics, Dynamics, Structural Analysis, or the alphabets. If you ask the teacher that God has appointed to you for help, He **will** teach and remind you! We'll talk more about this later.

As children of God, we must realize that we do everything as representatives of Jesus Christ. *God is more committed to your success than you are!* You know why? Because when you are His child and you succeed, He gets the credit! People glorify Him through you.

God is indeed your father. And, oh! The joy and pride a father feels when his children excel! The Holy Spirit will teach you, but you've got to be willing to do the work and study. You've got to be *willing* to learn. I believe that if you're willing to roll up your sleeves and do the work, God will break protocols just to make sure that you succeed!

Ben Carson, in his book, *Gifted Hands*, narrated the story about how he almost flunked a crucial exam, but a few hours before midnight of the day of his exam, he prayed and cried out to God to help him. After praying, he spent the next two hours studying and cramming as much information as he could. As he narrated his experience in the book, God showed up in his dream and gave him hints on the questions that would appear on the exam the following morning; and also gave him the answers! That's how incredibly awesome our heavenly Father is. But be careful...Ben Carson's grace may not be the same as yours! God does as he pleases. He might decide not to show up just to teach you a lesson. So, do your work...*study*!

2. Excellence is a habit:

In life, everything affects everything else. Because we don't always feel the effect of our actions immediately, we tend to believe that this statement is not true. But indeed, everything does affects everything else.

Excellence is a thing of character. And people of excellent character command great respect. People revere them a lot! If you can push yourself to turn your academics around, and turn your grades around, chances are very high that your success in the area of academics will propel you to strive for success in other areas of your life – say, your relationships, career aspirations, etc.

I heard Jim Rohn – a wonderful life coach, educator, and entrepreneur – once say, "Set high goals for yourself; not for the thrill of their accomplishment, but for what it will make of you to accomplish them." So, he was basically saying, the goal you set doesn't matter as much. What matters is who you'll have to become to accomplish those goals.

The same principle applies to academic excellence. You should work hard to excel academically **because of the person you'd have to become to excel**. In order to turn your grades around, and become an excellent student, you'd have to change into a new person – adopt new habits and change a few things about the way you currently do things. All these changes that you'd have to make to the person you currently are, are what's most important, not the grade itself!

These changes will alter your character and make you a person of excellence. And here's what's magical about this process: once you've grasped this concept and changed your character, you'd have become a whole new person! A person who will then begin to do everything you set your hands on with a measure of excellence that you never thought possible! You would have revolutionized your entire life by using your academic life to cultivate that character of excellence. This is what's important...not so much the "getting straight A's" aspect!

I hope you're getting excited about all the things you're going to take away from this book. Hang on! We'll touch more on these changes later.

3. You build a reference point for your brain:

You know, once you've walked through the fire without getting terribly burned, every other surface you walk on won't seem to be that hot! Or say, if you fight a

UFC fighter and live to tell the story, then, that bully in school that walks around giving people wedges will become a wimp to you.

The same thing applies to your academic performance. *If you can get yourself to turn it around, there is no other problem you'd face in life that you won't be able to rise and solve.* Academic struggles might seem so little, but if it were, how come a lot of people are still failing? How come those people who aren't doing so well in school won't get themselves to pick up a book such as this one to figure out how to turn things around? So, you see? It's not as easy as it sounds!

When you get yourself to excel this time, it becomes your brain's reference point for turning a poor performance around. This attitude will help you when you face other obstacles in the future. You can then say to yourself, "I've done it before and I can surely do it again!"

4. You owe it to YOURSELF to excel:

This is the most important of all the reasons why. It's that one piece of the puzzle that holds all the other pieces together! This is very crucial because even God will not force you to shine. God will never force you to do anything! So, ultimately, the ball is in your court. I mean... it's always been.

I said in the introduction that you're smart. I know this because everyone is smart, but ***very few of us take the time to cultivate and reveal that genius in us.*** The fact that we don't all make the effort to reveal that genius in us doesn't erase the truth that it is there – within each one of us – waiting to be awoken. And I'm not trying to sound deep or anything. I really believe it. As I type this, it's about 2AM in the morning. My eyes are burning, and my body is doing all it can to let me know that I need to "hit the sack", but I keep pushing myself because I believe you need this! I believe in that genius you have trapped inside of you. I also believe that following the practical steps outlined in this book will, hopefully, help you unveil it.

You owe it to yourself to excel! I mean...if you can, then why not?! It's a different story if your academic excellence was a total impossibility. But it's not! It's possible! You can turn your grades around. You can cultivate the character of excellence. You owe it to yourself to discover the boundaries of your abilities. You owe it to yourself to stretch to the limits of your abilities to become the best you could possibly be. If all it will take is your commitment to excellence and following the practical guides given in this book, you owe it to yourself to discover how smart you really are, and how far your intellectual capabilities can really take you.

Moving Forward

I hope you've gathered enough "Why's?" Please feel free to add more to the list we've discussed above. You know yourself. You know what reasons might motivate you even more effectively. The reasons we've discussed above are the ones that I know will strike a nerve in all of us – we can all relate to them.

Having gone through the reasons why I believe you should study and apply the techniques and practices given in this book, let's get to work!

"People with goals succeed because they know where they're going."

- Earl Nightingale

Key Question:

- Do you have a target you are trying to hit?

14 SETTING GOALS

Chapter Two

Setting Goals

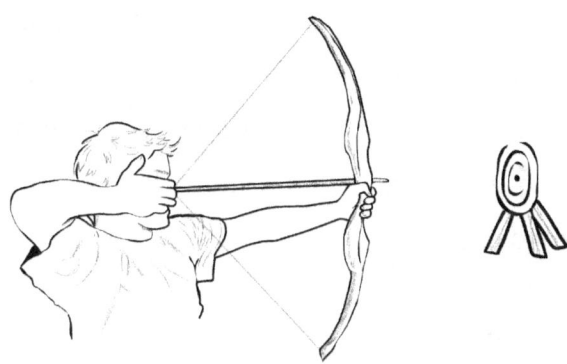

The Drift Zone

Let me ask you a question; and please be very honest in your response. How many times have you caught yourself drifting along in a class - i.e. going to class just because you must be there, skipping some classes to log a few extra hours of sleep after a long night of doing "only-God-knows-what"? I remember a guy back in college who showed up for an exam hung over! This dude very well knew that we had an exam that morning. But then again, why blame him, right? Why would a lecturer schedule an exam on a Friday morning – after the officially appointed clubbing night!? It was the lecturer's fault for sure - I blame him, too!

So, back to answering my question...Yes! I found myself there several times. I still remember some lectures that I gladly passed out in. The lecturer kept going on and on...and on, saying things I couldn't understand, so I put my time to better use – snoozing! We've all been there, and I am no exception.

Why We Set Goals

What are goals really? Goals are simply targets that you set for yourself and commit all your energy to meet. For us to feel alive as human beings, we need to have a sense of growth and progress towards a set objective! Setting goals gives us just that. It gives us something to look forward to and work towards.

Setting goals – whether academic or otherwise – helps you to define exactly what you really want and will also help you know when you've achieved it. You know, saying, "I want to do well in school" is good. However, when it is said without knowing exactly what "doing well" means to you, it becomes pointless. ***You must properly define your "objective" so that you can align your efforts and know clearly what you're working towards – and know when you've achieved it.***

Back in middle school, I never set goals. I'd go to school just to catch up with friends, play around and try as hard as I could to get the attention of the ladies. That's basically what I was all about - and I really sucked at the "getting the attention of the ladies" part! I'd give girls my lunch money – or in some cases, my cab fare – and then walk home! Can you believe that?! I'd give them my money to enjoy themselves, and then have to walk home! Oh, and just to give you an idea, we lived more than 25 miles away from my school! But then again, you wouldn't expect anything less from a middle school boy who desperately wanted to be liked by the ladies. Girls cost money!!

But you see, all that changed in high school. In high school, I met some of the most intelligent minds I'd ever met. These people helped me with the inspiration I needed to turn my academic performance around. We'll talk more about this phase of my life much later.

So, setting goals and academic targets every semester gives you a target that you must check your performance against, during the semester. You must keep your eyes on your target in order to make sure you hit them!

How to Set Goals

Again, this is a crucial step in the process of achieving academic excellence. You have to set a target to work towards. Now, of course, this target is going to vary greatly from student to student. One person might say, "I'm going to walk out of this class with an A." Another might say, "I've heard people say this class is so tough, even the smartest people I know find it very difficult; I won't mind getting a B." Yet another person might say, "I've heard people say this class is so tough, even the smartest people I know find it very difficult; so, I won't mind getting a passing grade and moving on."

I've been in classes where I said something similar to myself. One of which was my senior design course (capstone) in the college of Aerospace Engineering at Wichita State University. We had to design, analyse, and build a remote-controlled aircraft. That course, by all definitions of difficult, was...difficult! So, I set a goal to walk away with a B grade at the very least. Once I did, that became the lowest I would permit myself to get in the course. Regardless of where you fall - whether you believe you're book smart or not – it's important that you don't stagger into the semester. So, set a goal!

Here are a few hints for setting your academic goals. Please consider these as pointers. At the barest minimum, put these points into consideration while setting your academic goals, ok?

1. Write your goals down:

There's a proverb that says, "A goal that is not written down is merely a wish." This is an important step in defining your academic goal every semester. Decide what your goal is, but then write it down. Decide on what grade you want to get in each course you're taking that semester, but don't stop there. Go an extra step and write it down!

You see, there's an incredible power that comes with writing your goals down. You concretize your thoughts when you write them down. You transform them from mere thoughts to tangible, physical items that you can almost feel. Writing your goals down gives them a form of life and makes them physical for you to see over and over again. Preferably, make a list of all the courses you're taking that semester and write your target grade next to each one.

Does this sound too deep? Then, let me break it down for you…just get a pen and paper and write the grades you want to get in your classes, that's it!!

2. Set high goals for yourself:

This is not just about positive thinking. Les Brown – a renowned author, motivational speaker, and entrepreneur – once said, "Aim for the moon, so that if you miss, you'll land among the stars." So, set high academic goals for yourself, and this way, even if you missed your grade-goal by a fraction, the next best grade will still be higher than what you would've scored if you didn't set any goals.

If you don't set grade-goals for yourself, you're essentially leaving your performance in the class up to chance. You're saying, "I want to pass this class, but I don't care how well".

Here's my personal suggestion: aim to score A's in all your classes. At the minimum, set the target at high B's. And of course, you would do this so that if by some major cosmic imbalance – such as procrastinating on some homeworks – you fail to hit your target, you'll hit the next best grade.

Set a goal to be on the Dean's List, or to join an honor society as a result of your grades. Or better, set a goal to graduate with honors. This was one of my goals while I was a college freshman. I had watched a few episodes of Prison Break and learned that the main character, Michael Scofield, who was a genius, had graduated magna cum laude from college. I admired his character in that show a lot, and so decided that I wanted to graduate with magna cum laude. Once I made that decision, it was engraved in my mind, and I spent the next several years of college working towards that goal. And I achieved it! I graduated college with a degree in Aerospace Engineering and a cumulative GPA of 3.72/4.0. Pardon my bragging a bit about this, it's practically the only thing I get to do with it these days. Lol...

3. Commit yourself to achieving your goals:

As you may know, the saying, "knowledge is power" is incorrect in so many ways. Here's a more accurate statement, "Knowledge alone is potential power. Knowledge **acted upon** is power!" Knowledge alone is mere information. When that information pushes you into action, that's when the real power is released!

This one is a no-brainer. There is no point in setting goals if you're not going to discipline yourself to achieve them. Reading this book is awesome. In fact, I'm happy you, or someone who loves you, bought it. I'm happy that you've bothered to read it this far. But merely reading this book and learning the concepts in it is not enough. I'm tempted to say it is "virtually pointless" ...unless you put the things you learn into action! Knowledge not applied is useless.

So, decide that you will do whatever it takes to achieve your academic goals. Of course, this will differ for different people. However, in general, you'll realize that the changes you'd have to make to achieve your goals won't be so drastic that you will not be able to follow through.

When I was in college, I adopted the habit of not going out to do anything extra-curricular during the week, until the weekend - starting on Friday night. If I had to attend an event, I didn't spend much time there. I'd typically breeze in, and breeze out! Not that I didn't enjoy the company of my friends, I did...a lot, actually. And when I had some more time to spare - mostly during the weekends - I loved being around them. But I had to hit the books. I had to pay a price to achieve academic excellence. And so must you! You won't sit by, eating popcorn and watching TV shows, and expect to get good-grades. NO! Come on...you know better than that!

You've got to put in some work, and discipline yourself to follow through for you to achieve your academic goals. I'm not criticizing hanging out during the week, it just did not work out for me. I'm not saying not to have a social life or hang out with friends. What I'm saying is: *there will be a price to be paid, so, be open to paying it.*

You've Set Your Goals, Now What?

Once you've set your academic goals, you've separated yourself from more than ninety percent of your classmates. You are well on your way to academic success!

Next, you should check your individual test, quiz, and project scores to make sure you're on track to achieving your goal. You'll have to keep your eyes on each individual grade from your school work, since they add up to determine what your final grade will be. A lot of students don't realize this: **your final exam doesn't determine your grade in a class.** *Failing a class usually happens way before taking the final exam.* A lot of people fail half-way through the semester - even before taking their mid-term exams!

The point here is: don't depend on your finals. The accumulation of your quizzes, tests, and projects tend to matter more than only your final exam. Messing around with your class work all semester long and expecting that your final exam grades alone will magically turn things around is self-deception. In fact, I remember back in college, some lecturers intentionally weighed the final grade so little compared to quizzes and projects, in terms of total course grade. By doing this, students who believe they can dance and play all semester long, and then pull off an "all-nighter" the night before the final exam to pass the class will basically be...yeah you guessed it, toast!

Don't Give into the Storyteller

You see, if you'll ever meet your "high" grade-goal, you've got to realize that **everything** matters. Every grade you get in class matters. *You should not take **any** homework, quiz, or test for granted with the hope that you'll make up for it later.* NO! Don't do that, you'll be biting your tail if you did. I know this sounds a bit simplistic, but boy can it get so easy to put off some of your work during the semester! I know that feeling. You tell yourself, "Oh! It's just another home work. We have fifteen home works in this class, this one won't hurt won't matter much." Don't give into that!

Generally, homeworks, tests, and quizzes are the easiest at the beginning of the semester. At the beginning, lessons are still being introduced and there's not much of background information to pile things on. However, progressively, they will get more difficult each time. So, if your lecturers say they would drop a few of your lowest quiz grades, don't skip any one homework, quiz or test, with the hope of making it up; because you don't know how much more difficult things will get.

It's safe to assume that the homework, quiz or test you're planning on skipping is easier than the next one that's coming up. With this in mind, get yourself to do it now, and to do it well! Don't say, "I'll make up for it later;" Because the upcoming ones might not be as easy for you to "make up for it." Hope you get the point - do your work NOW!

Toward the end of my high school years and all through my college years, I was privileged to tutor and mentor a variety of students – my peers and other students. In high school, I particularly enjoyed teaching the ladies. Once I had learned to apply some of the things we are discussing in the book, and turned my academic performance around, I started getting quite some attention from the opposite sex. All of a sudden, they now "loved the way I explained complex concepts." Oh please! Spare me the heartbreak! Where were they before I became smart, huh?! Ppfftt...For my fellas out there...remember, remember, remember.... intelligence has a certain appeal with women. Don't ask me why, it just does!

Having tutored, and mentored quite a number of students, I've noticed this trend: **most students waste the first half of the semester playing, and then spend the latter half trying to make it all up.** Don't be like that! Don't give into the storyteller in your head. Don't let the lazy bum in you take control of your actions. Don't be like everyone else. Start the semester strong and keep yourself in check to make sure you finish strong! Do all your homeworks, quizzes, and tests to the best of your ability. Don't "hope to make things up later." Because that "later" might not be around the corner.

"Dates that come around every year help us measure progress in our lives. One annual event, New Year's Day, is a time of reflection and resolution."

- Joseph B. Wirthlin

Key Question:

- Can you tell what your grades will be before the end of the semester?

Chapter Three

Keeping Score

Don't Trash It

L et's now get into the details and talk some numbers. Roll up your sleeves and come along with me!

At the beginning of every semester in college, lecturers in every class will hand out a syllabus. This syllabus usually contains the topics that would be covered throughout the semester, the course policies, grading scales, and the allocation of the points in the class. The syllabus would also tell you the number of homeworks, quizzes, and tests you'd have in the class – and of course how many points each one's worth.

Most students tuck this syllabus in their textbooks or throw them away right after that first class. I know this because I was the ringleader of the group that would throw it away. I didn't know better then. In hindsight, I advise you, do not be like me. That syllabus is the rubric that will guide you in calculating your scores for the class during the semester to make sure that you don't fall off track. Keep it handy!

Determine Your Wiggle Room

Somewhere on the syllabus for each course you take should be the grading scale for the class. This grading scale would look something like this:

A: 90– 100%

B: 80 – 90%

C: 70 – 80%

D: 60-70%

F: <60%

Depending on your school, and your major, these ranges will vary a lot. Certain schools have the plus-minus grading system – I hate those! And for some courses, the grade range to score an A could be as high as 93% and above. In the Aerospace Engineering Department at the university I attended – Wichita State University – the range for getting an A in most classes was 93 – 100%.

But whatever the case may be, it is important that you understand what the range for getting your grade-goal is. Because this will help you understand the amount of wiggle room that you have throughout the semester.

This wiggle room is the number of points that you can afford to lose without falling out of the range to hit your grade-goal. For instance, if you set a grade-goal to get an A in your Biology class, and the grading scale is A: 90 – 100%, then you know you have about 10% wiggle room. This means that the sum of all the points you will lose from your home works, quizzes, and tests must not be over 10% of your total grade.

Keep Track of Your Current Standing

What this wiggle room concept implies is that whenever you get any score back, you have to check how that score affects your standing in the class. You can't just tuck the paper away and not bother to check. You have to know how much of your wiggle room you have used up. This will help you know how much extra work you must put into your remaining assignments, quizzes, tests, and projects in the class.

For instance, if the syllabus in your Biology class reads:

10 Homework – 1% each (total of 10%)

5 quizzes – 6% each (total of 30%)

4 tests – 15% each (total of 60%)

Notice what we talked about earlier – the final exam is worth just 15% of your total grade, while the rest of the class work's worth about 75%. So, if you're relying on your finals to be your come back, you're in for a huge surprise!

Let's say that you've turned in your first batch of assignments, sat for your first round of quiz, and taken your first test in the Biology class and got these scores:

Homework 1, 2, 3 – 5/10, 7/10, 9/10

Quiz 1 – 13/20

Test 1 – 75/100

These scores obviously show that you've been snoozing during lectures thus far in the semester. They are above average, but not good enough if you want to hit your grade-goal of getting an A in Biology.

Let's do a little digging to determine how much of your wiggle room you have used up.

Homework: (5/10 + 7/10 + 9/10) * 1% = 2.1 of 3%

- i.e. 3 of 10 homeworks at 1% each

Quiz: 13/20*6% = 3.9% out of 6%

- i.e. 1 of 5 quizzes at 6% each

Test: 75/100*15% = 11% out of 15%

- i.e. 1 test of 4 at 15% each

Wiggle Room Used Up: (3 − 2.1)% + (6 − 3.9)% +... (15 − 11)% = 7%!

So, you see, there's no possible way you'd be able to make that A (90-100%) if you've already lost 7% at this point in the semester! This means you have just 3% to lose before you miss your grade-goal. And going the entire semester without losing 3% isn't exactly very realistic.

This is a straightforward calculation. Don't let the numbers and symbols scare you. All you have to do is check to see how much each of the grades you get back affects your total grade – since you know the individual contribution of each assessment. *This will help you keep track of your work and know how much extra work you need to put into your studies; and what scores you'll need to make on your remaining assessments.*

Alternatively, what if your scores looked like this:

Homework 1, 2, 3 – 7/10, 9/10, 10/10

Quiz 1 – 18/20

Test 1 – 90/100

These scores elicit the observation that you're starting off strong. You might have had an average score on your first homework, but you picked your behind up and did better in subsequent ones.

Digging into the numbers to know how much wiggle room you have left, we'll get:

Homework: (7/10 + 9/10 + 10/10) * 1% = 2.6% of 3%

Quiz: 18/20*6% = 5.4% out of 6%

Test: 90/100*15% = 13.5% out of 15%

Wiggle Room Used Up: (3 – 2.6)% + (6 – 5.4)% +... (15 – 13.5)% = 2.5%

You see the difference? Now, you stand a better chance to make your grade-goal since you still have about 7.5% left to play around with. *All it takes is for you to keep track of your grades. And based on the feedback you get from your grades, determine how much extra work you need to put into your subsequent work to meet your target grade for the semester.* But you certainly can't be passive about keeping track of each grade and expect to magically achieve your grade-goal.

Finally, let's say you're just a nerd! Biology is so easy for you and you have nothing to worry about at all. Well, for one thing, your name wouldn't be Ugo Njoku because I despise Biology! But let's just say you're that good at this course and, hence, your grade turns out to be this way:

Homework 1, 2, 3 – 9.5/10, 10/10, 10/10

Quiz 1 – 20/20

Test 1 – 98/100

Checking your wiggle room, we get:

Homework: (9.5/10 + 10/10 + 10/10) * 1% = 2.95% out of 3%

Quiz: 20/20*6% = 6% out of 6%

Test: 98/100*15% = 14.7% out of 15%

Wiggle Room Used Up: (3 − 2.95)% + (6 − 6)% + ... (15 − 14.7)% = 0.35%!

Congratulations! You're a nerd! You see that if you had scores such as these, you could afford to go dancing for a while and not have to worry about Biology?!

Back in college, while working as a tutor in the college of Engineering, I would put each of my students through this exercise to assess where they were in terms of grades during the semester. So, they'd be aware of their current standing in the class and know how much extra effort to put in, and what grade to expect from the class.

I know, I know! It all seems like too much planning and too much work. Once you get a hold of this, it'll become second nature to you. Remember we already established that *excellence is a thing of character*. It's not something you just pick up. You must deliberately practice it. So, don't be weary in carrying out this little exercise ok!

It is sort of ironic, but in every class, you'd find both the nerds we talked about and the average students we analysed first. It happens in every class. Often in college, I had to find a way to turn my performance in a class around in order to meet my grade-goal for the semester. And I discovered that one of the most efficient ways of achieving this turn-around is to link up with a person in the class who seems to have it going seamlessly. We'll discuss this more later in the book.

Moving Forward

Remember that the things we talk about here will only be useful to you if you actually put them into practice! So, get started as soon as possible to assess where you are in each class, and keep close track of your grades with every assessment you receive. To make sure you're doing better in exams and retaining more, let's take some time to investigate studying and how best to do it.

"It is a mistake to think that the practice of my art has become easy to me. I assure you, dear friend, no one has given so much care to the study of composition as I. There is scarcely a famous master in music whose works I have not frequently and diligently studied."

- Wolfgang A. Mozart

Key Question:

- How do you get the most out of your time in front of your books?

Chapter Four

Don't Just Read...Study

Reading Versus Studying

There is a great difference between reading and studying. In fact, they are not the same thing! I mean, I never knew the difference myself. So, I used to sit around with my friends in a loud and busy atmosphere and scan through the words in my notebook or textbook. Come to think about it...textbooks?! Pppftt...I never used those! I glanced through my very incomplete notebooks. But whatever the case was, I didn't study! I highly doubt the legitimacy of the fact that I even read. All I know is that I saw words – barely knew what they meant though.

Differences Between Reading and Studying

*The **major** difference between reading and studying is: **the level of attention you pay to details.*** When you read, you typically don't take the time to think things through. You just pull the meaning and significance of the words you're reading from your memory bank and keep going. It's very possible to read without understanding – I mean, kids do this a lot! Reading is rather effortless, especially as you advance in age. And in most cases, you don't care enough to do any extra research or snooping around for additional information regarding things that you don't completely understand.

For instance, when you come across a strange word while reading, you seldom drop the article or paper and look for a dictionary or go on Google to look up that particular word. In fact, if you're anything like me, unless you're being forced to read that article, you'd read ahead of that word and based on the context of the sentence, figure out it's "supposed" meaning. You can't deny this...I know you do it also!

On the other hand, studying is an art. It takes time. If you study without understanding, you'd be like a majority of the college students out there today. But, ideally, when you study, you are supposed to strive for understanding. You're supposed to pay attention to details, in order to completely understand the material in question. **_When you study, you are answering the "why?" and "how?" questions in reference to the information presented in the material you're studying._**

For instance, if you ever watch the TV show *Bones* or any other investigative show, you'd realize that there is a trend to all of them. And I pray you make out some time to watch a little TV. Life shouldn't be all work and no play! Well, here's the trend: they typically start off with events that lead to a murder. Then, forensic agents show up to collect a whole bunch of data from the crime scene. The medical folks collect samples, while the law enforcement folks go snooping around and questioning suspects. But for the entire show, you'd realize that what the medical folks are looking for is the "how?" of the murder, while the law enforcement folks are looking for the "why?", and maybe the "how?" as well. That's also what you do when you study. You're investigating to find out the "how's" and "why's" things are the way they are.

How to Study

Remember I said studying is an art? Yes, that's why this chapter is dedicated to giving you a few studying tips and techniques on how to study effectively, or help you hone your studying abilities.

Tip # 1 - Search for Patterns and Trends:

Learning how to do this changed my studying effectiveness forever. I still use this in my working life today - i.e. it works outside the walls of college. I find myself identifying trends and patterns in order to efficiently store information in my memory.

During the process of my academic "rehabilitation" in high school, we had to prepare for a physics test – I remember the setting of the class room and everything.

We were going to be tested on the Kinematic Equations of Motion. Now, because I had started changing my studying habits and had decided that it was time to improve my academic performance, I knew I had to master the equations of motion. I knew this because I realized that most of the problems we were solving were heavily based on the equation.

Like most students at the time, I was focused on taking notes - writing frantically, everything the teacher put down. I never really took the time to understand what the equations meant, or what the teacher was talking about. And this is another reason why you have to learn to study...so that you can make sense out of what your teacher says in class - at your own pace.

Well, when I got home and started studying for the test, I applied this technique to remember the equations. I sort out patterns that would help me remember each equation. I starred and concentrated on the equations for a while, seeking out things that would stand out to me as a pattern. I didn't want to memorize, because doing this meant that, if I forgot one thing, I'd progressively doubt myself and forget the rest of the equations as well. So, I sought out letters or trends in all the equations –

something that they all had in common, or the similarities between their derivations. I did this for a while, until I found a pattern.

The R-A-S

Let me briefly mention this. There's a part of your brain called the Reticular Activating System (RAS), whose function is to tell your brain what to notice and what to block out. Of course, you know that if your brain picked up or noticed everything going on around you in a given moment, you'd probably go crazy! So, your RAS helps tell your brain to notice only the things that are significant and helpful for you to accomplish your task. It helps your brain notice things that are relevant or significant to you.

For instance, have you ever bought or checked out a shirt, or a car, or a phone, and all of a sudden it seemed like the shirt, phone, laptop, or a car was now all over the place? Well, guess what? It always was! But your brain never noticed it because your level of awareness of the item was not very pronounced. But once your level of awareness of the item was increased, your RAS enabled your brain to spot it everywhere.

When I Found a Pattern

Well, after a while of looking for a pattern while studying those equations, I found one! I realized that the method of derivation of the equations were similar. The first equation was derived by taking the first derivative of the distance equation, and then doing a little rearranging. The second equation was derived by taking the first differential of the first equation and doing a little rearranging and so on. And they were all arranged in a similar manner too. So, instead of memorizing all three or four equations, all I memorized was the distance equation, and then I could use the pattern I had found to derive the other equations if I ever forgot them in the exam hall!

Once I became aware of the existence of patterns and how effective they are, my studying habit was transformed - I didn't have to cram anymore! I used the same technique to understand complex equations in college, and I do the same thing today. *Learn to seek out patterns and trends in whatever you're studying.* **It is a very efficient way of storing complex information you have to internalize, without cramming.**

My Cousin Chigo

I recently had an experience that very accurately portrays this concept of searching out patterns. One evening, I was hanging out with my cousin, Chigoziri. He was 11 years old at the time. I walked into the kitchen – where he was trying to put together some ramen noodles delicacy for himself. He saw me and asked, "How old is sister?" They call their eldest sister, "Sister," as a sign of respect. "I want to know how old I will be when she becomes 30 years old," he continued. Totally random! But he's always been analytic.

Being me, and trying not to give him the answer without teaching him some lesson in the process, I told him, "Well, for us to know how old you'll be when she's 30, we have to know how old she is now and how old you are, correct?" He nodded in agreement, and we set out to figure out this complex algebra!

I went on to ask him, "OK, how old is sister now and how old are you?" He said, "Sister just turned 20 years old and I'm going to turn 11 years old soon."

I smiled and asked him, "Well, so if sister is 20 and you're 11, then how old will you be when she turns 30?" He pondered for a bit, doing the calculation in his head. And then looking up at me, he said, "hhmm...when she's 30, I'll be 21!" Noticing the pattern, he said, "So, whenever she turns a zero, I turn a one!"

He didn't just get the answer to the question he had, he figured out a pattern! His mind told him, "If she's **20** and you're **11**; and will be **30** when you're **21**; then most certainly, whenever she turns a zero, you'll turn a one!"

That's exactly what I'm suggesting you do. ***Don't just memorize the material in front of you when you study; study it for patterns.*** *Find out... "IF this is this...then THAT will be THAT. But is it going to be like this always?" Does it always apply? Does it apply for special cases only - only when this and this happen?* What associations can you make with the new information you just learned?

How to Identify Patterns and Trends

Ask yourself, "What do all these have in common?", "Are the arrangements similar?", "Are the derivations similar?", "Do they sound alike?", "Do they have the same first letters?", "Do their letters come together to make a word – you know, like an acronym?" Really search and trust that your RAS will lead you to a trend.

Patterns usually come in the form of cause and effect - *i.e. when "this" happens, "that" usually happens; when I see "this", then I'd usually see "that" afterwards.* **It also comes in form of grouping things and searching for similarities and repetitions** - *i.e. recurrence of things.*

As I pointed out earlier, *looking for patterns involves understanding how final equations or statements were derived; that is, understanding the logic that led to the final product that others would merely memorize.* **Don't always memorize; understand the "How?" and "Why?"**

This is especially important for exams. Don't just take what your teachers give you on review and study guides. Study them for patterns. Even if the teacher changes the format of the questions, you won't freak out because you understand the concepts. Once you get the principles, you'll always have the upper hand...always!

Tip #2 – Repetition is Key:

Have you ever heard the saying, "Repetition is the mother of skill"? Sure you must have at some point. What it literally means is that the more you do something, the better you become at it.

The Learning Curve

Research has revealed that: *the performance or ability of an individual increases remarkably with repetition over time.* So, the more you do something, the easier it is for you to do the next time. Until you get to a point where you don't even have to think about your action; you just do it. Like riding a bike. Once you've got it, you don't need much effort.

Repetition in Studying

I have personally found this to be very helpful. *When you study a material and don't understand it,* **don't** **progress!** *Do it again! Go through that material over and over again until it makes sense to you.*

In certain materials, the information that lie ahead help clarify the ones that come before. While in others, if you don't understand the information, there won't be any point in moving ahead, because the information that lie ahead build on the previous ones and get complicated as you flip the pages forward.

So, my advice is to go over the information multiple times until it begins to make sense, realizing that each time you go over it – looking out for patterns, paying attention to details, and trying to relate it to things that you already know – you'll understand it a little better. You might have to read through a section several times. You might have to read through a page over. Or you might even have to read through an entire chapter to make sure that you truly understand what it's talking about.

But whatever the case may be, ***don't move forward until you've completely understood the subject matter that is being discussed*** in the section, page, or chapter. I mean, what's the point of moving forward when you don't understand where you're already at, right?

Tip #3 – Study Your Monster Class Everyday:

I have found that no matter your level of education – high school or college - there's always a class that seems the most difficult to grasp compared to the other classes that you're taking that semester. This particular class will disinterest you the most. If the class seems very difficult to understand, you'd develop a form of hatred for it.

I had a class just like that every semester in college. Even in middle school, I had subjects that I despised. And because I hated them so much, I couldn't afford to spend my time studying them. Let alone try to understand what the teacher was blabbing about in class! In middle school, it was Mathematics!

I hated Maths so much! But as they say, "hate" is a strong word; maybe "despise" will work better! I mean, the mere thought of it scared the heck out of me. And because of my disgust for the subject, I learned not to like the teacher as well. I mean, if you're going to despise the message, chances are very high that you wouldn't be in love with the messenger either!

This unseen battle between Math and I continued until a few weeks before I had to take my exit exam from middle school. This exam was cumulative – it included the topics we had covered between the end of elementary school and that point in our middle school. I mean, I wasn't excelling academically back then, but at least I knew I could find my way around other classes. But Math though? Nah...didn't have a clue!

The Advice That Changed It All

One day, I happened to be with my mom when she decided to pay our pastor a visit at his home. I don't remember us setting out to visit him; she just decided to stop by to see him, since we were close by. Who knew that such a "spontaneous gesture" would turn my academic life around?

A few minutes into our visit, my mom went to use the bathroom. So, she stepped out leaving just me and the pastor in the living room. Clueless as to how to relate to a youngster like me, or what on earth to discuss, he decided to ask me about school. I reported that I was doing great in school – ppftt...I lied – but that I was really struggling with Math. I remember him smiling and telling me his own stories with the dreadful subject.

But then he gave me an advice that changed it all for me. He said something in the lines of, "Math is not very difficult. Study it every day from now and you'll see what will happen." Just about then, my mom walked in and asked what we were talking about. We gave her the gist of it and the spot light shifted from me. They went back to having their "adult conversation" which I wasn't the very least interesting in.

Now, because my pastor was a man I respected – and still do respect – I took his words to heart and decided to try out his suggestion. The next day, I found an algebra textbook and started studying it. I still have a mental picture of me studying the book. It was an old, algebra textbook with brown covers. It also had answers to the exercises in the back. And I think they were all worked out; I can't remember. I'd ingest as much information as I could for a period, and then go out to play.

The first day I tried it, it wasn't fun, neither was it easy to understand the symbols and everything written in the book. But my pastor said it would work, and I believed him. So, the next day, I got back to it. I studied about forty-eight pages or so the first two days. And of course, the more I studied it, the more I understood what was going on. They wouldn't all make sense to me, but the information was sipping in and unclogging my brain!

The Pay Off

I continued studying that book religiously every day. It all started to make sense! I started getting the symbols and how to work them. My brother and sister saw me spending a lot of time studying the book. I wasn't playing as much anymore because I was so engrossed in figuring things out from the book. I reported my progress to my father, at one point and he seemed so proud of me. This fuelled my desire to learn more. He encouraged me to keep going, and even promised me a gift – oh dang! I never redeemed that gift!

I also reported my progress to my pastor and he, too, encouraged me to keep going. My mother was also very supportive. So, I guess it does take a village to raise a child, huh? With all the morale boosting going on around me, I kept studying that textbook every day! And as you would expect, because I had been engrossed in Math so much, I started getting a hang of it. And before long, I became very good at Math!

In fact, in my second year of high school, some friends and I represented my school in an international Mathematics competition. My mom bought me the Math textbooks that I asked for – even though it cost her quite a bit of money. For that competition, I studied a variety of Math textbooks in order to prepare myself. I went for the competition, which involved students from many other high schools in the country. I remember the exam being full of people - all bright students!

The students which were among the top ten performers in the competition appeared on the evening news and received a certificate on live television. And guess what? I made it! I was awarded a Pan African Mathematical Olympiad certificate, and appeared on the evening news! I was so ecstatic. That was the first big pay-off of my hard work in Mathematics. I had, with the help of God, turned that monster class around in my favour!

Of course, my newly found love for Math helped make studying Aerospace Engineering possible. I mean, you really can't navigate through the sciences smoothly without learning how to, at the barest minimum, tolerate Math. Learning to love Math also helped me excel in other classes that I had troubles with, and it helped me cultivate a "can-do" attitude towards my other monster classes. With this can-do attitude I had cultivated, amongst other factors, I had such an exceptional academic performance in the university I attended in Malaysia – Sunway University College – that I was awarded the Western Michigan University Presidential Scholarship without applying for it! I also ended up graduating college with a minor in Mathematics. Imagine that!

At different points in my college career, I won a bunch of awards, which are all good things. But come to think of the fact that the process that led me to win those awards, receive the scholarship, have a great academic performance in college, and a great career - in Engineering and entrepreneurship - began with one advice which led me to conquer one monster – Math. It's amazing.

I'm very humbled every time I reminisce about how far I've come. Truth is, I owe all my successes, triumphs, and who I've become to God. I'm just a dumb boy who God allowed to learn how to be smart - practically. I'm really humbled.

How this Applies to You

Now the same concept applies to your own monster classes. ***If you want to excel in your monster classes, you must make time to study them every day.*** You don't have to spend hours. Just a few minutes will do. But make sure you look into, or at least glance through that subject every single day.

What happens as you engross yourself in the subject is that, you'll find it easier to understand. And all you need is a trigger. *A trigger happens at the point when the lecturer says something, or you read something that relates to a single point that made sense to you while you were studying the subject.* That's all you really need; because starting from that point, your brain will begin to interweave everything else to make sense to you. That will be your epiphany. It will inspire you to study and strive to figure everything else out. More things will begin to make sense to you, thereby creating a self-fuelled process which will lead to your understanding and enjoying that class. I know this because it has happened to me more than once!

So, don't question the reasoning. Just do it! Study that monster class every day, even if you don't completely understand what you're studying. In his book, *Outliers,* Malcolm Gladwell points out that to be exceptionally good at anything, you must spend about 10,000 hours doing it. While you might not necessarily need to hit this number when it comes to school work, it certainly helps to be exposed to the information you need to learn a few more times than studying for an upcoming test or quiz.

Here's one last point to ponder under studying your monster class: **when you've conquered this class, you would've created another reference point** to *look back at to build your confidence.* You can now look back at this class in the future when you're faced with a monster challenge and say to yourself, "I've done this before, and I can do it again!"

Tip #4–Study to Know, Not Just to Pass Exams:

This is perhaps the most important advice anyone could ever give you. This is why studying patterns is so important. You put in the effort and work to study and identify patterns so that you can retain the information for the long haul.

Don't Be Caught with Your Pants Down

Retaining the information for the long haul is crucial for your success, especially for your core classes – i.e. your math and science classes if you're still in high school and want to study engineering, medicine, or any other major that is science oriented. If you're already in college, then it is important to study to know when it comes to Statics and Dynamics classes for an Engineering major; or Biology class if you're a pre-med or Biology major. *The reason why this is so dang important is that* ***every subsequent class you take in your core areas of study will always build on the knowledge of the previous lower level class.***

Your lecturers will assume that you'd thoroughly covered the subjects in the previous class – the prerequisite class – which you needed to pass to get into the more advanced class. So, what would happen if you merely went through the class studying for each test and didn't retain the information as you walked out of the exam hall? You'd be uumm...basically caught with your pants down! Don't be caught with your pants down! See what I did there? Ha-ha.

Why Study to Know?

Don't cram! Study to know, so that even years after you're done taking the exams, the information will remain locked inside your brain. And if you forget anything, a little review will bring it all back to mind.

When you study to know, you won't have to study as much for upcoming comprehensive tests. For instance, if you're taking a class that the final exam is comprehensive – i.e. covering all the topics covered in the class all semester long – or the tests are combinations of the things covered on your quizzes, then it would be very wise if you studied for the long term. This way, you wouldn't have to study intensely more than once. You'd study for the quizzes and tests and then merely go over things one more time in review for your exams.

I know we won't always be this meticulous in our methodology and study habits, but bear these ideas in mind anyway. But if you can follow through with them, then do it! *Study to acquire knowledge; not just to pass your exams.*

As we discussed earlier, each advanced course builds on the knowledge of its prerequisite. For instance, Math 111 builds on the knowledge from Math 110, and so on. And for the most part, most lecturers assume that you know the information from the previous course. So, studying to know and for the long term will help ensure that you're prepared for the more advanced classes that will build on the knowledge of your present class.

Guess what happens when you cram just enough information to pass an exam? You forget everything once you're done with that exam! A friend of mine back in college, named this concept, "Chew, Pour, Pass, and Forget!" So, you load your brain with information for the exam, you sit for the exam, hoping to God that most of the things you crammed show up on the exam. If you're in luck, they will and then you'd pour everything just as it was written in the books, make a decent grade or even ace the test, and then…forget it all! Now, guess what you'd have to do for the upcoming comprehensive exam? Study it all over again! What a pain in the behind, huh?

The Payoffs

Aside the confidence that comes with knowing that you have the information in a course down pat, and excelling in subsequent courses, there are other more lucrative benefits to studying this way. Here's one: when I was in college, I worked as a Physics tutor in the college of engineering. On that job, I was paid quite an impressive hourly rate to teach freshmen and sophomores Physics. I was a senior in college at the time. But guess when I studied the information I taught them? In my high school and freshman years!

I never had to review much to teach them. Whenever I saw an equation, I'd remember when I studied it. With the knowledge I had acquired about four years before, I'd break things down for them to understand. I was paid for what I knew! I was paid because I took the time to study for the long term; not just to pass the exams I had at the time!

Real Talk

The reason why I suggest you do this especially for your core classes is because those are the classes that are the most important to your major and your discipline. I mean, you don't necessarily have to study to know the information given in your World Music general education class if you're a Biology major. In the ideal world, yes! you might have to study it all, be good at it all, and know all the information. But, being "real" with ourselves, there are certain classes for which holding in as much information as you need to hit your grade-goal is just sufficient.

No one should be unreasonable and say, "Study to know World Music for the long term" when you're a pre-med student. I mean, if you're a music enthusiast or a Music major that's alright. But if you couldn't care less about World Music, then I suggest you focus your attention where it is really needed – in your core classes. Study World Music, get that "A" in the class, forget it all and just move on!

Tip #5 – Doing Homework is NOT Studying:

This is another point that most high school and college students don't understand. **There is a huge, in fact, massive difference between doing your homework and studying.** The only time when it might count as studying is when you make out time to study *before* completing your homework. But then again, who are we kidding here, right? Most of the time, you just want to get the dang homework over with and move on to watching movies and hanging out with friends.

I think this is an important point to review because I've found that a lot of students confuse completing assignments with studying. Especially high school students. They spend a very long period of time doing their homework and never put everything away to concentrate on assimilating the "work."

You see, if you're not focusing on internalizing the methods of completing the homework, you're not studying. Now, is it possible to do the two simultaneously? Yes, in some cases. I say so because I've taken a class or two where I meticulously studied my notes before completing my homework. I did so with the mentality that I was catching up with my school work, and it worked! That helped me have a better idea of what was going on in class up to the point of the homework. I understood what I needed to know to complete the homework. But is everyone like Ugo? Nope!

How Do You Work Around This?

How to work around this is pretty simple in my opinion. Just tell yourself the truth. When you're completing your homework, you're not really paying much attention to anything else but what would help you get the work done. *So, if you can,* **study everything and then use the ones you need for your homework.** *However, if you can't, then I suggest you make out time during the weekends or some other time to really study.* But please...please...please...don't you convince yourself that you're studying just because you're getting your homework done. You're not!

Tip #6 – Watch the Atmosphere Around You:

I've found that some people don't mind studying in a busy and noisy atmosphere. I used to say that about myself, too. That was before I understood the difference between reading and studying. *For you to truly study the content of the material in front of you, you need as little distraction as you can get. If it's at all possible,* **don't allow any external distractions while you study.**

I know that, especially in college, when you're at the library or in your study halls, study rooms, or whatever name you call it at your school, your friends might see you and come by to exchange a few pleasantries. And that is acceptable. However much you can, control the amount of distractions you have while studying.

Effective studying requires that you involve your mind and your entire focus in the process. Remember, earlier we stated that you have to pay attention to details, as you seek out patterns and go through the rituals that you need to get the information into your memory. You'd agree with me that it would be difficult to accomplish this with friends coming by every five minutes; or with your phone buzzing with text messages every other minute.

Hints on Eliminating Distractions

Put your phone on silent mode, not vibrate. And put it away for those minutes that you're trying to log some studying time. Try to find a place where a lot of people won't see you and come by to greet you. If your library has multi-levels, then go to a level that's not where the entrance is. Because when you sit close to the entrance, you're sure to see and be seen by the people that are coming in and leaving.

I mean, sitting at the entrance has its benefits. You get to check people out as they walk in and leave, but then again, you'd be paying too much of a price to feed your eyes! Don't do it! Go and hide someplace where you won't be seen. A few minutes to yourself, to enrich your mind and prepare yourself for excellence in life is not a bad investment.

Back in high school, there were a few spots that I identified as good hideouts for studying. As an exit exam out of high school, we were required to take a comprehensive exam covering all the information presented in high school. It was a very serious exam. It determined whether you'd be going into college or not. It was an international exam, so the board that set the exam knew nothing about which topics were covered in any one particular school. The exam was standard for all schools and there was no mercy involved! But thank goodness, by the time I got to this point in high school, I had learned to study and God had helped me transform my academic life. So, I was ready to put in the work required to ace this exam. But in order to excel though, I knew I had to study, and I couldn't do that with people playing and distracting me.

I found a few spots on the school campus where I could go hide out and work when I wasn't in a playful mood. Also, in college, I found a few spots in the library where people didn't come by a lot. I'd go hide out in those spots and do some serious work; especially if I was lagging in my classes. But generally, I'm not a very big fan of libraries. I think they are way too quiet. Because of this discomfort with the silence in the library, I studied at home a lot. I found it more relaxing, and I could take as many breaks as I needed.

Back in the dorms, we had a few study rooms. But you know how it is; people come in and make noise and all that stuff. So, generally, I'd go to study rooms if I needed to study but was very tired, because I knew that if I studied in my room, I might be tempted to fall into bed and snooze. Also, if I had a group meeting, or needed to study in groups, then I'd go down to the study room. But whenever I went out to the study rooms, I was sure to have my ipod, laptop, and phone with me to play music and look "busy", fending off unnecessary interruptions in the process.

Set the Mood

I don't know about your particular preferences, but I know some people don't like studying in total silence. I, for one, am one of them...thank God for cloud music!

It might be helpful to introduce a little controlled distraction when you study, like music or weather conditioning tracks. Yes! Weather conditioning tracks. There was a semester where I was required by my English teacher to write an eight-page essay on a subject of my choosing.

In order to set a relaxed mood to complete my work, I went on YouTube and played rainforest sound effects while I wrote the paper. It was quite hypnotic. And it worked! I totally felt like I was in the amazon rainforest writing this paper - water falls, birds chirping...the whole nine yards! You should try it sometime, when you don't want to listen to music. It will help relieve stress, too. It creates such a serene, relaxed, and therapeutic ambience. And since it's YouTube, you could decide to select multiple sound effects; maybe, rainforest, or amazon, or rain with thunder. But try it out.

But if you're music lover, then by all means use that. Plug in your headphones and lose touch with your surrounding as you delve into the pages of your notes or textbook. I suggest you buy noise cancelling earphones...so you won't be distracted by the noise in your surroundings, and your music won't be distracting the people around you as well! Boy do I hate it when people are listening to their taste of music – which might be completely contradictory to mine – and I can hear everything loud and clear. No! You listen to your music over there and leave me in peace...I don't want to hear any of it!

Music and Subliminal Messages

Have you ever noticed how commercials are becoming more and more sexual? You'd hear smooth jazz music and see a man with a well sculpted body, or a lady with a very attractive figure, and expect to see an advertisement for some exotic island someplace. Instead it turns out to be the ad for a kitchen sink draining fluid! What about a commercial that comes with smooth jazz music and virtually naked people advertising an antidepressant, for which they go ahead and list more than a thousand side effects? And the question is: what is the connection between the sexually appealing music and scenery, and the product they're selling? And the answer is: Nothing! Absolutely nothing!

What advertisers are doing is taking advantage of your subconscious mind. They know that when they play you real smooth jazz like that, they essentially put you in a state of partial hypnosis, which opens up your subconscious mind to the message they're sending you. And since the subconscious mind is the deep-seated storage for humans, you'll tend to retain the information they're passing along to you for a longer period. And by relating the product to sex, you'll tend to be more attracted to it - if you've ever watched an Old Spice commercial, you'd realize why Isaiah Mustafa never leaves his shirt on while shooting those commercials! These are called subliminal messages, and this technique of advertising is called Subliminal Advertising.

What does this have to do with your studies, you ask? Well, that's about the same thing I suggest you do while studying: *play relaxing and soothing music on your musical device while you study.* What this does is, just like those commercials, it'd open up your mind to receive a great portion of what you're studying; and you'd retain the information for longer.

Yes, you might be scared it will make you sleepy. And it might. But in all the years I've done it, it didn't particularly send me to sleep, but helped with the assimilation of what I was studying.

Tip #7 – Take Breaks:

While studying, be sure to take breaks. *Don't go for long stretches without taking a few minutes to freshen up and relax your brain.*

Don't Be That Guy

I know what it feels like in those moments when you sense all hell is breaking loose. You have a test on Monday, Tuesday, Wednesday, and Thursday. The test on Monday covers three chapters, the one on Tuesday covers two chapters, the one on Wednesday covers five chapters, and the last one on Thursday covers just four chapters. It is now Saturday on the weekend before your most exciting week, and you're not done studying for the test on Monday - let's not bring up the rest of the tests.

Well, here's a tip I've come up with to help you through this period: "DON'T be that guy!" Don't be that person who waits till the weekend before a heavy week to start serious preparations. Pray for that person. Encourage him to keep pushing on...but DON'T be him!

It might seem like I was exaggerating with the exam schedule just described. But to be honest, some people have it bad like that sometimes. I used to have exams back to back to back. In such times, you want to go crazy! You believe your lecturers have definitely held a meeting behind closed doors and decided that they want you dead, and they want you dead in a week. Ha! So, how do you tackle such a situation?

Spread It Out

If you've ever been in that situation before, don't allow yourself to get there again. Lecturers usually announce tests and quizzes at least a week before the scheduled exam date. They are required to give you ample time to prepare. I realize that you might have things going on that are zapping up a good deal of your time. *During such a crunch time as the one described above, where you have back-to-backs,* **you'll need to** *cut off every other activity that will distract you from your school work.* Devote, at minimum, the week prior to your back-to-back exams to studying hard for them.

This will allow you to spread out your work a bit. When you prioritize your activities – with school being at the top of the list, you'll be able to work hard to get ready for your tests before the "last-night-cramming" alarm goes off. **Use the night before your exam to review the material to be tested, not to study new information.** I can think of two reasons why you would want to take this advice:

1. So that you can take breaks while you study:

Like I said earlier, this is very important, so that you relax your brain for a bit before going back to studying. Relaxing your brain will help you assimilate more information. It will help you be more receptive. When you spread out your work properly, you can afford to leave your books for a little while and go chat with a friend for a few minutes. You can go make a real quick phone call and "holler" at a pal. Or you can take a really quick walk. Anything that will help you take your mind off the books.

When you get back to it, you'll have a fresh perspective to the subject you're studying. You would have allowed the things you studied to sink in and become more rooted. And when you get back, you can see how much of the information you've actually understood. So, take breaks in-between studying!

2. To avoid diminishing returns:

Diminishing returns is the inevitable end of studying in a hurry. *Diminishing returns happens when your brain has become saturated* - because you're throwing a lot of information at it without giving it time to process them. **This causes you to start forgetting the information you already knew and understood.** This usually happens when you have to cram a lot of information in no time.

It's been estimated that the world's fastest computer is still extremely dumb in comparison to the capacity of the human brain. So, it's a fact that your brain can take all the information you are trying to shove into it. The only problem is that you're trying to shove it all in at the same time...in one night. No. No. No! If you do that, at some point, your brain will be tired of receiving new information so fast. Without allowing it time to process them, it would literally stop receiving; and if pushed further, will crash! Especially if you're also running on little sleep. Please don't push yourself to a meltdown. Spread out your work, as much as possible.

If you crash, you won't be able to take the tests, and the class would sit for the test without you. You would have messed up whatever wiggle room you had left, and probably dropped below your target grade. You might even flunk the class, depending on how far behind you'd been. And since the school stands to makes more money if you repeat a course, they'd be happy to enroll you in the course again the following semester!

Therefore, regardless of how you choose to look at it, the smarter move is for you to spread your work out as much as you possible, and do the best you can, given the amount of time you have.

Additional Notes on Studying

Asides the obvious reasons for studying, i.e. to ace exams, and become smarter, there are other subtle reasons why you'd want to cultivate the habit of being serious with your academics. Here are some of those subtler reasons:

1. You don't always understand the teacher:

Yes, that's true. Most of the time when we're sitting in the classroom, listening to the teacher, and taking notes, information goes by so fast that we don't always understand everything in real time. Somewhere in-between trying to grab everything that is being said, taking down notes or highlighting PowerPoint slides, and checking out the outfit of the person sitting next to you, you'll invariably miss a few things the teacher is trying hard to explain. And that's very understandable. I, too, don't support being a perpetual nerd. It's OK if you don't get everything in class...as long as you go home and study.

You begin to fail the moment you start becoming nonchalant about any aspect of your

school work. A nonchalant attitude will make you care less about a lot of things – assignments, quizzes, and test – which will ultimately lead to the demise of your academic excellence.

So, why should you study when you get home? Here's one answer: *in order to understand those things that the teacher explained and wrote down in notes that eluded you in class.*

I learned to do this in my junior year of high school, and I've not stopped it till today. I learned to sit in class during the day and listen to the teacher go on and on about things I didn't necessarily understand. And then I'd go home, eat, do chores – if I have any time, take a little nap and then wake up in the middle of the night to study - one to two hours will do the trick. While studying at these hours, I typically have little to no distractions. I'm able to assimilate better.

There's also something about waking up at night to study that draws us close to divinity. Earlier in the book, I mentioned being taught by the Holy Spirit. These moments of tranquillity make it convenient to learn from

Him. He'd lead you to the correct thought process to yield the understanding you need.

2. Transform the information into your own frame of understanding:

We all understand and process information differently, and at different rates. This explains why certain subjects seem to resonate better with you; as a matter of fact, you grab them during the lectures. While others seem to elude you at first, but with practice, you'd get good at them. But someone else in your class – maybe one of your friends – needs help in both areas. Meanwhile, another one of your friends completely understands all the concepts. That's just how it is.

We all understand things by taking the information as it is presented, and interpreting it into the frame that works for our brain – *maybe still pictures, or motion pictures, or patterns.* ***We then store the interpreted form in our memory.*** Because no two persons have the same rate of comprehension and frame of understanding, it's important that you study at **your own pace** when you get home.

Don't be intimidated by all the people that got it in class while the teacher was still explaining it. They got it and didn't fail to let the entire class know, by asking a whole bunch of questions that ended up throwing you off balance some more. Yeah, whatever…show offs!

Pay no attention to them haters! Just grab as much as you can while you're still in class, and then take very comprehensive notes. We'll talk more about taking notes in the next chapter. With the notes and the little information that you picked up in class, your studying time later will be very productive, and you can show up for the next class session ready to rock 'n' roll.

Oh! and by the next class session, those folks who thought they caught everything in the previous lecture, but really stored the information in their short-term memory and failed to review them after the left class that day, would've forgotten most of it. And now guess who gets the opportunity to shine, huh?! Yeah… YOU!!!

Moving Forward

Ok we're making progress! I'm glad that you've come this far! I am really proud of you. It's about 7:00 AM right now and, I started writing at about 10:00 PM last night. I've not slept all-night! And that is because I feel the connection between me and you as I write this. I feel like this is really going to make a difference in your life. And if it does, then it's worth my putting all my strength and mind into. I pray your hard work is rewarded!

Next, we're going to discuss more concepts that will help you transform your academic performance. Be sure to apply these techniques that we're discussing. Like I've never failed to remind you, they'll only work if you put them into practice!

"The content of most textbooks is perishable, but the tools of self-directedness serve one well over time."

- Albert Bandura

Key Question:

- Is it possible to know more than your teachers?

Chapter Five

Embrace Your Textbook!

A Universal Law

Dreading textbooks is an unspoken universal law! I'm yet to meet a single student who loves to read their textbook just because they feel like it. So, don't feel bad if you don't either! As a matter of fact, majority of the students that I've met and talked to are not exactly excited about the idea of studying textbooks.

The irony of this situation is: unless you're in middle or high school, where you don't have to buy your textbooks, you typically are required to buy some form of a textbook in college. And these books are usually not cheap! Back in college, I remember buying books in the high hundreds of dollars. In 2012, there was an electrical engineering textbook I saw priced over $500! And I know some majors have even more ridiculously priced textbooks.

So yeah, textbooks are expensive! Even if you found a way to buy used books, some of them are still pretty pricey. And the pathetic thing about college bookstores is that they sell you these books at such ridiculous prices and then buy them back from you for very little! Rip-offs!

Now here's the age-old question: if you spend so much money to buy these massive volumes of pages, why wouldn't you make use of them? Well, you could correctly argue that the answer to this question lies in the very question itself – textbooks are massive, and often overwhelming to attempt to read.

But just like everything else in life, you'd have to embrace it. You'd have to face your fears and make your textbooks your best friends if you want to excel academically. I wish there was an alternative. But this is one of those times when you'd have to bite the bullet and form a habit that is not something you'd adopt excitedly.

My Textbooks and I

You see, as I briefly mentioned, learning to study my textbook was one of the first skills I had to learn in order to turn my academic performance around. I learned this in middle school, and the habit stuck with me through college, even up to this point in my career. Here's what I've concluded: ***If I must study, I'll study the one thing that makes all the difference.***

That's exactly what a textbook is. Even though most of them are scary looking – and every so often, some are written in a very-hard-to-understand manner - they are still valuable to turn your academic performance around. You wouldn't believe it! Till today, I still study a few things from textbooks and other resources. Thank God I learned to suck it up and embrace them!

What Textbooks Should You Study?

This is a question that invariably arises whenever I mention the benefits of studying textbooks to students. They usually pull the "But I have about five classes! I can't keep up with studying the textbooks for all five classes!" That is absolutely true. It would be insanity to try to keep up with studying all your textbooks, going to lectures and taking notes, then doing your assignments and all other forms of school work. At this point, no one's even talking about having any kind of life. Just keeping up with the school work is a lot to carry!

In response to the "what textbooks should I study question," I would say: **study, very meticulously, the textbooks of the classes that are the most difficult for you to understand.** Seems very obvious right? Wrong! A lot of students find it easier to complain to lecturers and fuss about how they don't get the information in class. They resort to complaining to their lecturers first. I'd say this is a wrong approach. The last thing you want is to create an impression that you're a lazy student, especially to your teachers. They'll become uninterested in listening to you and might deem you "unserious."

*You want to go to your lecturer **<u>after</u>** you've studied your textbooks and still don't get the concepts...not before.* This way, when you walk into their office, or you walk up to them after lectures, you can tell 'em how much independent studies you've done. They won't tell you this, but in their mind, they'll start perceiving you as a serious student and might cut you a little slack. **Every teacher wants to see that students are interested in learning the material they present in class.** *Even if your grades are not reflecting your efforts, they'd go out of their way to help you work things out.* I know this because I did it a couple of times in both high school and college. This subject is covered in another book - *Ace It!* In that book, we'll cover the art of acing exams, including how to win over your lecturers and utilize them as resources!

For now, let's take a look at some of the reasons why it's very beneficial to study your textbooks. Come with me!

Why Study Textbooks

Here are some of the reasons, or benefits, of embracing your textbook. Please read and consider them carefully. Debate them in your mind and ensure they makes sense to you.

Reason #1 – Your teachers don't know everything:

Yes! Contrary to what most of them would like to admit, they don't know everything! As a matter of them, most of them are as clueless about some topics as you are sitting right here in their class. I had a number of lecturers who blanked out in class while trying to describe something that seemed complex. They, too, became confused! I mean, they're supposed to be the ones "teaching" us these concepts. And there they were, all puzzled and perplexed about why things didn't add up!

Have you ever observed how a good number of lecturers tend to stick very closely to their notes? How about the ones that stay glued to their PowerPoint slides? Some lecturers blatantly refuse to answer questions that they know will lead them off track from what they originally "planned to deliver" for the day. This is because they just don't know it all.

This is where your textbook comes in handy. *Your textbook **bridges that gap** between what your teacher lectures about in class and what you need in order to understand the material.* This perspective helps you value your textbook.

Study What Counts

I mentioned earlier about studying the "thing" that counts. Yes! Your textbook is that thing. You see, unlike your teachers, the authors of textbooks conduct *very* extensive research to verify the information contained in these textbooks before they are published. No author of a serious textbook will put just his opinions on a subject down on paper and publish. No, no, no...I don't even think he'll be able to find a publisher that will accept his manuscript. Because if the information he presents is found to be false, then even the publisher has to answer a few questions.

So, you can be rest assured that the information the authors of your textbooks present are – at least to the extent of currently verifiable data – correct. Therefore, your textbooks contain waaaay more information than your teacher could ever convey in one course. When you study textbooks, you amass an enormous amount of knowledge that your lecturer may have never shared with you.

Most textbooks are written by more than one author - i.e. the combined knowledge of different experts made readily available to you. So, if you'd get yourself to read these textbooks, you'd be drawing from the knowledge of the best minds on the subject that you're studying. You'd be seeing the subject matter through their eyes. Now, if you'd add this perspective on the subject matter – from the authors of your textbooks - to the one presented by your lecturer, you'd have a plethora of ways to understand the same subject. And who's to say, maybe the way the textbook explains it will click better for you than the way your teacher explained it in class.

Imagine being in a room with Einstein teaching you his infamous, *Theory of Relativity*. You would have to somehow open up and learn the subject matter, right? Because hey! It's Einstein! He knows his stuff. Well, it's about the same effect those authors should have on you. They're well-grounded on the subjects they're discussing in the textbook. So, give it a shot! Open up and soak it all up.

Reason #2 – Class notes are the teacher's interpretation of the textbook's material:

Understand this: your class notes are merely your teacher's interpretation of what the textbook author(s) wrote. Why would you want to settle for tea spoons of knowledge when the ocean of knowledge is right in front of you? But that's what happens when your teachers give you notes in class – they go to the ocean and get you a teaspoon worth.

Most high schools and universities require teachers to make their own notes for the course they are teaching. Your teacher is, therefore, obligated to study the textbook that's to be used in the course – and maybe other supporting textbooks – to gain an understanding of the material (s)he will present in class. Everything they teach you in class is based on *their* own interpretation of what the textbook is trying to convey. But why rely on only your teachers understanding?

I'm in no way trying to discredit the teaching skills of any of your lecturers. Most of them work hard to present the information the best way they can. Others show up to class and confuse you even more! Every student - college and high school alike - has had at least one of such teachers.

Glued to Notes

As a matter of fact, I realize that certain lecturers stick super close to their notes, and set quiz, test, and exam questions from what they taught you in class. Therefore, I'm not saying to count your teachers off! I'd be deceiving you if I said such a thing.

I also realize that because the quizzes, tests, and other materials might cover only the topics that the lecturer covers in class, you will not see the relevance in going back to study the textbook. I know that students don't like opening their textbooks. I understand your hesitation to the idea of studying more than what you absolutely must.

However, I'm making these suggestions to you because I believe that you're serious about your academic success. I believe that you really want to excel. That's why I'm saying this. *You study your textbook because you want to gain a more in-depth understanding of the materials you're discussing in class, especially when you don't understand what is going on during class sessions.*

That's why I suggest that you go back to your textbook: **to read up the rest of the materials that your teachers didn't think were relevant to be put in notes.** *These might actually help trigger your understanding of the topic.*

Embrace the Source

It's amazing how much information you can grab when you get yourself to open your textbook. I know most of them are very voluminous and seem to have a lot of information. But most of the time, when you start studying them, they're really not difficult to understand. I would greatly suggest going back to this source that even your lecturers go to frequently. I know I've stressed this point a lot, but it's just that important.

When I Was Deceived

Well, I wasn't actually deceived. I was just plain dumb back then. When I was in middle school, I became friends with a very smart boy – let's call him James, for anonymity. James loved reading. While the rest of us struggled to understand what was going on in class, he read a variety of novels - for leisure.

Looking at him without being forewarned about his nature, you would easily mistake him for a very unserious and carefree individual. But in reality, James was far from that. He was one of the top students of our class set. I later discovered the secret of his excellence, but I lost quite a bit of ground in the process. I was so busy following his lead in school that he very conveniently, how-be-it unknowingly, led me astray!

We once took a chemistry test which most people agreed was very difficult. But you know how it is, there is always a group that tend to excel even when everyone else is complaining. Well, I didn't belong to this group at the time. James did, however, this time he was too busy playing around that he didn't properly prepare himself for the test – and neither did I! When we got our papers back a few days later, it turned out that I had performed better than James did. I got a few points above a zero, while he got a flat zero.

I remember feeling bad about my score, but at the same time, feeling good because I scored higher than he did. When he got his paper, he was very disappointed and, being in a very solemn state, said, "I'm going to make this up. I'm going to cover up for this mistake." I was with him at the time, and I was feeling bad about my score, too. So, I made a similar resolution. I said something quite close to what James said. I said, "Yes! I'm going to turn this thing around on the next test. This will not happen again!"

After we had finished having our moment, James went home and dug into his textbook, while I went home and caught up with my cartoon episodes. We both had incomplete class notes, and we also had the textbook for the Chemistry class. But I thought making a resolution to turn things around was all it took. Ppfftt...I told you I was dumb back then!

I never knew about the secret to James' success, but this experience taught me about its effectiveness. Whatever it was that he was doing was working. Because come the next test, we both walked into the exam feeling confident that we would ace the test; but only James walked out smiling. I was bummed! I barely knew anything!

It was later in my high school years that I understood what James did. You see, after we bummed our first test and decided to bounce back on the second one, James attacked his textbook! He chewed that thing up. He was already a smart and hardworking student, with very highly developed studying habits. While I, on the other hand, was…uumm…yeah, you get it! I studied my class notes which were incomplete and went in barely understanding the material. Of course, when the result came out, I failed yet again, while James aced it. No kidding. I was left at the bottom all by myself!

The Lesson

I told you this story to highlight the point that I've made a few times already: if you embrace your textbooks and study them with understanding, you will not only catch up with the concepts that you missed during in-class lectures, you'll learn enough to make you excel and turn your academic performance around!

Reason #3 - To cultivate the habit of studying textbooks and other self-help materials:

This reason is perhaps one of the long-term benefits of learning to study your textbooks now. Like we already talked about earlier, **cultivating the habit of independent learning is far more important than acing an exam.** And that's exactly why I suggest you adopt this habit now.

While you're in school – whether high school, or college – you go to class, and sit still listening to your teachers go on and on and on. Once class is over, you pick up your things, chat with a few friends, and off you go. This only works in school though. However, most people after they graduate from school sit around waiting for a teacher to come along and tell them which books, websites, and other resources to use to better understand the things going on around them. They are in for a rude awakening, though, because that teacher just won't come along!

If you desire to be successful, and to excel in life, you must learn to search for information by yourself. This time, there are no grades to be on the *lookout for, only the quality of your life – which in any sane person's opinion is more important than grades!*

Even while practicing in the field, medical doctors – in many occasions – still have to go back to their textbooks to review some information. Yes! My dad is a medical doctor, and I remember seeing lots and lots of textbooks in his office whenever we went by his office. I've also read about other doctors who, when faced with a difficult case, would go back to conduct some research before prescribing anything to the patient.

Engineers also do the same thing. There are several instances when, as an engineer, you're faced with challenging problems that you might have forgotten the basic information on how to tackle. What do you do in those times? You go into research mode. You go back and read all the information you can find on the subject. And once you feel like you've gotten a hang of it, you can head back to work and solve the problem.

Even today, I still do a lot of independent studying. There are certain projects or tasks that you would have to complete where it is not acceptable to walk up to your boss saying you don't know how to get the things done.

That's not what you're paid to do! In those cases, I apply the studying techniques I learned and used through the years. I go back and find as much information as I can find on the subject and study them! I go on YouTube, use Google; whatever resource I can lay my hand on. And this process is not much of a hassle for me because I learned these techniques. I learned to love the process of studying.

As we pointed out earlier, teachers still must do a lot of studying to make their notes and to know their information enough to teach it. They just can't stand up there and not have a clue what they're talking about.

In order to be successful in whatever field you decide to play in, you can't stop learning and growing. After you collect your diploma and leave the gates of your school, you still have to consciously cultivate the habit of studying.

Personal Development

When I graduated from college with my first degree, I had a lot of odds against me. I didn't have any internship experience – a very big mistake that I made. Internships are very important. They help you rack up experience in the field, while still at college, so you don't have to worry about having "no experience" upon graduation. Well, no one taught me that.

Understanding the constraint that not having any experience placed on me, I needed to find some avenue to spice up my resume. And to accomplish this, I decided to learn how to use some softwares which were widely used in the industry. I also had to take some certifications to help boost my market value and improve the appearance of my resume. To do this, I relied heavily on my ability to study and conduct personal research. What if I hadn't learned to do this while I was in school?

So, learning how to study your textbook really does pay off in more ways than getting good grades in school. If I had any advice to give college students at this point, it would be: **learn how to study and, at the very least, do one internship while at college.** If you must skip a semester to do your internship, do it! Absolutely, try completing at least one internship in your field of study before graduation!

What to Do If You Still Don't Get It

If you study the assigned textbook of the class and still don't get the material, then I'd suggest you try different authors. You might find that you get the drift of one author more than the other. Alternatively, you could go to your school's library and find an older edition of the textbook you're currently using in class; or find an entirely different material which was written in a manner that appeals to you. When you go back in editions, you understand more of the original intent of the author(s); and hence, the material. I have found this to be very helpful.

During my undergraduate studies, we were required to take at least two masters level courses before graduating. As an Aerospace Engineering senior, I decided to take the Aerospace Engineering grad-level course, *Finite Element Analysis*. Well, quite contrary to what I expected, the course was difficult...very difficult! I had a very hard time grasping the material in class - it all sounded like gibberish to me. At some point, we had a lengthy assignment due and a test coming up. So, I had to understand the information in order to be able to complete the assignment and prepare for the test.

Just like we're discussing now, I tried studying the assigned course textbook but didn't understand a thing! Then I went to the school's library and found the version of the textbook that was written in the 1980's. This happened in 2012! I went back to the older version of the textbook and re-discovered the original intent of the author. I found that the older textbook explained things in much better details than the newer edition. So, I used the older version to understand the "once-so-difficult" concepts.

How to Know When You've Studied Enough

Up to this point we have discussed studying your textbook, why you should study them, how to study them, and all that good stuff. Now, very briefly, I want to discuss when to stop studying your textbooks - or studying in general.

The answer to this question is a no-brainer: **you should stop when the information starts becoming recurrent.** This might happen after a few pages, or a few textbooks. It doesn't matter, just keep going until you hit that point when the information makes sense beyond every reasonable, and conceivable doubt.

But you see, the difficult part is not *when* to stop studying textbooks, but it is how to get yourself to *start* in the first place. That's why most of this chapter dealt with that. I hope that you've accumulated enough reasons to decide to give it a try, and hopefully, make a habit of regularly studying your textbooks.

The God Factor

In conclusion. After doing everything we've discussed in this book, you need God's help. I put this section last because **I'm a firm believer that spirituality and Christianity is not opposed to skill, study and discipline.** You can pray from today till next year, and probably even add fasting to it. But if you don't sit down to plan, act on your plans, and constantly review to find opportunities for improvement, it would be better for you to go have yourself a full buffet instead of spending all that time hurting your knees in prayers!

If you proclaim to know God, then you must realize that God is disciplined. Prayer is not a replacement for labor. You are supposed to spend countless nights studying, *in addition to* praying that your classes will go well. It is important that as representatives of Jesus Christ on the earth, we ensure that we don't sound ignorant and unlearned when we speak. We must not seem undisciplined in our actions. **God hears us when we pray and helps us when we work. We need both!**

Wrapping Up

I am very proud of you for coming to the end of this book. I hope you learned a lot from it. I expect that you would go beyond reading these words to putting the things we've discussed into practice. I'm excited to hear what happens and the results you get from putting these into practice.

Stay in touch! I love receiving feedback and learning about the things going on in your world. Feel free to follow us on social media @**neugenleaders** and go on our website ***www.neugenleaders.com*** to learn about the release of *Ace It!* It will cover practical steps on acing exams and becoming a star student, among other things.

Until next time...bye now! :-)

ACKNOWLEDGEMENTS

I consider myself extraordinarily blessed for the things I've been given and for the people I've crossed paths with whose lives positively influenced mine, and ultimately enabled me to write this book.

My wife, Elizabeth, is at the very top of that list. Baby, thank you so much for reading the manuscript, and proposing several changes. Thanks also for allowing me to work very long hours. You're one heck of a superwoman and I'm blessed to have you in my world. I must also thank our son, Solomon, for being a strong, and cheerful boy. Thanks for not breaking daddy's laptop while he worked - even though you came very close many times.

My special thanks goes to the editor, my dear friend and sister from another mother, Chidiebere Eze. She read the manuscript, and in her characteristic perfectionist manner, proposed amendments to provide better clarity to my content. Thanks a lot for your help, Chichi! My beloved best friends, Adanna Njoku and Mary Onyarin, thank you for believing in me and encouraging me to carry through with publishing this work. Dare Fenwa was also a believer and gave me the motivational pep talk to make noise about this book; thanks, buddy!

Most of the content shared here was written in 2013. During this time, I was living with my uncle Ndubuisi Njoku, his wife Ify Njoku and their family. They have become second parents to me. I appreciate the love they showed me while I lived with them - and continue to show me till today.

I owe thanks most of all, though, to my parents, Dr. Emereuwaonu and Dr. (Mrs) Laetitia Njoku. Even though I left the nest at an early age, you inculcated a sense of independence and responsibility in me years before I had to travel halfway around the world to start my college career. You made a lot of sacrifices to make sure my siblings and I had a shot at the good life. A life in which we had the freedom to engage in the pursuit of our dreams, ambitions and happiness. I'm forever grateful.

ABOUT THE AUTHOR

Ugo Njoku is a youth speaker and the founder of NEU Gen Leaders, LLC – a youth leadership development organization committed to helping teenagers discover their life's identity and mission. He studied engineering – at both undergraduate and graduate levels – and currently works at a fortune 500 corporation. Ugo currently lives in Indianapolis, with his wife Elizabeth, and their son Solomon.

www.ingramcontent.com/pod-product-compliance
Lightning Source LLC
Chambersburg PA
CBHW071406290426
44108CB00014B/1704